Teen Guide to Credit and Debt

Craig E. Blohm

San Diego, CA

About the Author
Craig E. Blohm has written numerous books and magazine articles for
young readers. He and his wife, Desiree, reside in Tinley Park, Illinois.

© 2017 ReferencePoint Press, Inc.
Printed in the United States

For more information, contact:
ReferencePoint Press, Inc.
PO Box 27779
San Diego, CA 92198
www.ReferencePointPress.com

LIBRARY OF CONGRESS CATALOGING-IN-PUBLICATION DATA

Names: Blohm, Craig E., 1948- author.
Title: Teen guide to credit and debt / by Craig E. Blohm.
Description: San Diego, CA : ReferencePoint Press, Inc., 2017. | Series: Teen guide to finances |
    Includes bibliographical references and index.
Identifiers: LCCN 2016018763 (print) | LCCN 2016022562 (ebook) | ISBN 9781682820803
    (hardback) | ISBN 9781682820810 (eBook)
Subjects: LCSH: Consumer credit--Juvenile literature. | Credit--Juvenile literature. | Finance,
    Personal--Juvenile literature.
Classification: LCC HG3755 .B56 2017 (print) | LCC HG3755 (ebook) | DDC 332.7/43--dc23
LC record available at https://lccn.loc.gov/2016018763

Contents

Credit Card Debt Has Fallen to a New Low

Credit card debt, as a percentage of total US household debt, has steadily dropped since 1997 and, in 2014, it reached the lowest level since 1990. This finding appears in the 2015 Nilson Report, a trade newsletter covering the card and mobile payment industries. In the graph, the blue bars represent growth in total household debt, an amount that equaled $13.5 trillion at the end of 2014. Credit cards accounted for only 6.5 percent of that debt at the end of 2014 compared with about 10 percent in 1996, when credit card debt reached its highest level since 1984.

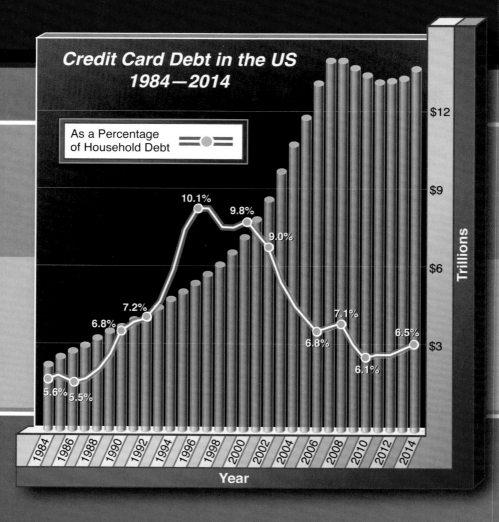

Credit Card Debt in the US 1984—2014

As a Percentage of Household Debt

- 5.6%
- 5.5%
- 6.8%
- 7.2%
- 10.1%
- 9.8%
- 9.0%
- 6.8%
- 7.1%
- 6.1%
- 6.5%

Trillions: $12, $9, $6, $3

Year: 1984, 1986, 1988, 1990, 1992, 1994, 1996, 1998, 2000, 2002, 2004, 2006, 2008, 2010, 2012, 2014

Source: *Business Wire*, "The Nilson Report: US Household and Credit Card Debt 2014," June 24, 2015. www.nilsonreport.com.

Chapter One

Credit

An online ad hypes a new version of Apple's iPad. A television commercial advertises a new, extreme role-playing game. Magazine ads showcase the latest designer jeans and splashy jewelry. In the world of commerce, these types of advertisements are often aimed at the approximately 40 million teenagers in America, whose purchases range from shoes and music downloads to fast food and concert tickets. Results of polls taken by several marketing companies and *Seventeen* magazine revealed that spending by and for US teens totaled $258.7 billion in 2014.

At the same time, however, many of the consumer goods that appeal most to teens are more expensive than they can afford. A teenager considering such a purchase has several choices. One is to simply do without the latest gadget or fashion accessory. Another choice is to save up enough money until he or she can afford to make the purchase. A third option is to spread out the cost of the item in affordable installments: in other words, to buy on credit.

Credit—the concept of purchasing goods or services

with the expectation of future payment—is not new. As early as 1300 BCE traders in ancient Babylonia were making business transactions employing a type of credit. Today millions of people use credit to purchase things that are necessary for daily living or that add enjoyment to life. Houses, furniture, cars, and family vacations are some of the many costly items that are likely to be purchased on credit. Without such financial arrangements, businesses would be forced to rely on cash-only transactions, and expensive items would only be affordable to the very rich. With credit, people can buy the goods they need or desire that would otherwise go unsold. In short, credit is an important basis of today's economy; without it, the economy would likely collapse.

Sources of Credit

For many people in search of credit, the first place they look is where the money is located: a bank. Most banks offer credit in the form of loans to purchase automobiles, houses, home repairs, and other big-ticket items that are usually paid for over time. Loans usually include a monthly fee, called interest, which pays the bank for lending the customer the money. For many teenagers, buying a car is often the first major purchase made on credit, a transaction usually referred to as financing the automobile. A bank will examine a potential buyer's financial situation before offering a loan. A good place to begin looking for a loan is a bank where the teen has a savings or checking account.

A savings and loan (S&L) company is similar to a bank and offers many of the same types of loans and other financial services. S&Ls deal mainly with home loans but often provide other consumer financing, such as auto

Is There Life Without Credit?

The signs of our credit-obsessed society are everywhere, from the boasting of a "low, low, low!" interest rate on television car commercials to the numerous credit card offers that fill American mailboxes with alarming regularity. With all the seemingly easy-to-obtain credit out there, is it possible to live without credit and debt?

Travis came from a credit- and debt-free family. His parents watched every penny, buying generic groceries, patching clothes, and limiting eating out to special occasions celebrated at the local McDonald's. The only debt they had was a mortgage, and they always made more than the minimum payment to shorten the life of the loan. Theirs was a lifestyle without credit cards, and the payoff for Travis was graduating from college debt-free.

Each family is different, and not everyone can live a life without debt. Also, there may be consequences of living without ever using credit, such as not building up a good credit history, which may be necessary when applying for certain jobs. But for those who have the determination to stick with it, striving for a debt-free life is a worthwhile goal.

loans. Banks offer these types of loans as well but also service corporate and government customers.

A credit union is another source for financing purchases. Unlike banks or S&Ls, credit unions are nonprofit cooperatives that are owned by the people who deposit their money with them. Their customers are members, and as a group they determine the policies of the credit union. Usually smaller than banks, credit unions offer their members car, home, and other consumer loans and can provide more personal service to their customers.

For those who are unable to obtain a loan from a bank, an S&L, or a credit union due to current or past financial problems, private finance companies are another source of credit. Loans from these companies usually carry a higher interest rate due to the higher-risk customers they serve.

For a teenager who has little or no income and no credit history, parents may be an ideal source of credit, if they are willing and able to make a loan. Borrowing from parents can help a teen learn valuable lessons about whether an item is worth paying for in installments, how interest works, and the importance of paying back loans without going to a commercial lender. Parents will set the terms of the loan, the amount of interest (or no interest, if they so choose), and a payment schedule that their teen can afford.

One of the most popular ways to get credit is the use of credit cards such as Visa and MasterCard. These cards are accepted at nearly all types of businesses nationwide, from a small local store to the endless variety of merchants that can be found online. Many individual department stores and specialty shops may also provide credit to their customers by issuing credit cards to be used for purchases in the store or on their websites. These businesses often provide special discounts or other incentives exclusively to their store cardholders.

"When I started working as a teenager, and when I eventually got loans for school, I went a little crazy with the spending."

—Yael, a college graduate

Cards issued by gasoline companies such as Shell and BP are useful once a teenager has started driving. Accepted for the purchase of gasoline and other items at their issuer's service stations, these cards have a low maximum spending limit, usually between $250 and $1,000. This can help teens learn to use credit cards sensibly without running up excessively high balances.

The Importance of Good Credit

Purchasing goods on credit can be beneficial for a teenager's financial future. Rasheed, a student at Barry University in Miami, Florida, was having trouble keeping his finances in order. When he began looking to buy a car, dealers told him that he did not have the necessary credit history to finance the purchase of a vehicle. By obtaining a credit card and using it wisely, he was able to begin establishing a good credit history.

Rasheed learned the importance of using credit responsibly. But when used unwisely, credit can lead to problems that may take years, or even decades, to correct. Some of these problems include developing poor spending habits, incurring fees for late payments, and going further into debt to pay off existing loans or credit card charges. These bad habits can mean serious trouble for a teen's financial future, making it difficult or impossible to obtain credit when real needs or emergencies arise.

The most important factor in assuring that a purchase made on credit will not cause problems down the road is paying back the amount borrowed promptly in accordance with the terms of the loan. Missing even one payment could negatively impact a person's credit history, making it more difficult to borrow money later in life, or resulting in higher interest rates on loans that are obtained. Missed payments can also cause lenders to add late fees to monthly bills, thus compounding

The Secrets of Credit Card Users

Most people consider how much they make and how they spend to be a personal matter, and they understandably keep their financial dealings to themselves. In order to get a glimpse of how Americans use credit, Gallup, one of the world's leading research firms, surveyed more than one thousand people about their credit habits.

The poll, conducted in April 2014, revealed that 48 percent of Americans always pay their credit balances in full every month, while another 16 percent usually do so. On average, Americans have 2.6 credit cards and carry an average of $2,426 of debt on their cards. These figures are lower than those reported during the 2000s, indicating that Americans are relying less on credit cards and paying them off faster than before. This may be due, in part, to the aftermath of the great recession of the late 2000s, when credit card companies raised interest rates.

So Americans seem to be saving more and charging less, which is good for both the individual and national economy. But even though people are relying less on credit, those little plastic cards will not be disappearing anytime soon.

the problem. College graduate Yael knows firsthand the perils of credit. In a story on the lifestyle blog *Yes and Yes,* she recalls, "When I started working as a teenager, and when I eventually got loans for school, I went a little crazy with the spending." But when she saw how miserable being in debt had made her mother, she worked hard to pay off her loans, becoming "officially student-debt-free (15 months after I started), and now [I] only owe $200 on my credit card. It's a beautiful feeling."

Many of an adult's most important expenses, such as cars and houses, rely on having a good credit history. Mistakes made early on, even as a teenager, can mark a person as unreliable, and therefore a credit risk, making the necessities of life more costly than they would otherwise be. As credit counselor Bruce McClary notes on the NBC News website, "We do see a lot of college students who get in trouble with credit cards and it carries over to later in life. Well after college they are still struggling to get out from under that mountain of debt."

Why Not Pay Cash?

Teenagers who work at part-time jobs or receive money from doing household chores may have enough money to buy many of the things they need or want with cash. A macchiato at Starbucks or a movie with friends is usually within reach of a teenager's spendable income. But often a teen will want to purchase something that is beyond his or her ready cash. This is where planning ahead can become important. Creating and living within a budget is a good way to avoid the necessity of buying things on credit. Opening a savings or checking account and saving up the money needed to purchase an expensive item is a good way to learn financial responsibility.

The ability to pay cash for everything is, unfortunately, a luxury available only to the richest Americans. Still, many everyday expenses can, and should, be made with cash. When standing in line at a store or coffee shop, it can be faster and more convenient to swipe a credit card or tap a phone at the payment terminal. But that is one of the big problems with credit: using it can become *too* easy. On the other hand, paying with cash has certain advantages. When handing money to a cashier, it is a reminder of the cost in real dollars of the item purchased. This can be easily overlooked when using credit cards, leading to overspending that can quickly grow into a financial nightmare. The decision to pay cash for most purchases requires careful balancing of income and expenses. Creating a budget is a good way to monitor finances, and developing the discipline to follow it will become a valuable habit.

Using Credit Wisely

Since paying cash for everything is an unattainable goal for most people, buying things on credit becomes a necessary alternative. The trick is to be smart in the way that credit is used. The majority of Americans need to use credit at one time or another in their lives in order to make necessary purchases, such as replacing a worn-out appliance, or dealing with emergencies that may arise, like paying for an unexpected illness or making needed automobile repairs. These are all examples of using credit wisely, but many teenagers find it difficult to keep credit spending under control. College student Vince, enticed by an offer of a free T-shirt as a premium, signed up for several credit cards. He intended to use the cards only for emergencies but soon found himself using them for more than just unexpected purchases. Soon he had amassed $15,000 in credit card debt, which was in addition to his college loans. Ultimately, Vince had to quit school and get a job to pay for the debt he had incurred.

> "We do see a lot of college students who get in trouble with credit cards and it carries over to later in life. Well after college they are still struggling to get out from under that mountain of debt."
>
> —Credit counselor Bruce McClary

The wise use of credit, whether in the form of bank loans, credit cards, or retail store accounts, is a foundation of good financial health. The teenage years are the ideal time for developing good monetary practices and avoiding the pitfalls that the misuse of credit can cause. A little early planning, learning about credit, and forming good spending habits can result in a lifetime of financial health.

Chapter Two

Credit and Debit Cards

It happens millions of times a day. Shoppers take their purchases to the checkout counter, and when the total is tallied they reach for a little piece of plastic to complete the transaction. The credit card, which first became a nationwide phenomenon in 1950, revolutionized the retail industry. No longer was cash a necessity: a small card, first made of cardboard and, later, of plastic, allowed people to buy things now and pay for them later.

Today's teenagers are no strangers to buying things on credit. According to one survey, 38 percent of college students had at least one credit card in their own name in 2016. And among those students, 23 percent had more than one card. Even students who did not have a credit card agreed that they are useful tools for building consumer credit. High school student Tori was excited to get her first credit card. In the book *The Complete Guide to Personal Finance for Teenagers and College Students,* she says, "Trips to the mall, the movies, out to eat—it was all going to be so carefree now!"

Credit Versus Debit Cards

Two basic types of cards can be used to make purchases in stores and online: credit cards and debit cards. The most popular type of credit card is the standard card bearing the name of a multinational credit card service such as Visa, MasterCard, or Discover. These cards allow users to purchase goods on credit at almost any brick-and-mortar store as well as at online merchants around the world. The banks that issue these cards use the credit card services to manage the millions of transactions that take place every day. With a credit card, the issuer is, in effect, loaning money to the user for the purchase of goods and services, with the expectation that the money will be repaid in the future. Like bank loans, credit cards accumulate interest on outstanding balances.

To many young people who are discovering credit cards for the first time, these little pieces of plastic seem like an ideal and enjoyable way to shop. In *Not Your Parents' Money Book* by Jean Chatzky, student Meredith was asked her opinion about buying things with credit cards. "It seems like magic," she said. "I always wanted one because then I wouldn't have to spend real money anymore. Then you're with your parents and you look and there's a credit card bill and you're like, 'Oh. . . .'" As Meredith learned, despite the convenience of using a credit card, the bill will always come due, and it has to be paid with "real money."

> "I always wanted [a credit card] because then I wouldn't have to spend real money anymore. Then you're with your parents and you look and there's a credit card bill and you're like, 'Oh.'"
>
> —Meredith, a student

The other basic type of card is the debit card, formerly known as a bank or check card. Debit cards are almost identical to credit cards, often displaying a Visa or MasterCard logo, but with the word *Debit* printed on the front. Unlike credit cards, which essentially allow use of a bank's funds, a debit card uses a person's own money. When a bank opens a checking account for a customer, along with checks, a transaction register, and a checkbook cover, the account's owner can also receive a debit card, which is linked to the account. When the card is used to make a purchase, the amount is immediately deducted from the checking account. This differs from using a credit card, where payment is not required until the bill is received.

For many teenagers, a debit card is a good first step toward learning about using credit wisely. Debit cards are easier to obtain than credit cards, which require either proof of the ability to make payments (such as a part-time job) or an adult cosigner for those under the age of twenty-one. Nineteen-year-old college student Dallas wanted a credit card, but his parents felt he needed more financial experience, and encouraged him to use a debit card first. "We know he's not ready," says Dallas's father, Curtis, a consumer advocate, on the NBC News website. "If he proves that he can be responsible with his debit card, we'll co-sign a credit card with him."

Types of Credit Cards

Although all credit cards may look alike, behind their shiny plastic surfaces there are differences in the way they operate and the extra features they provide. Standard credit cards, like Visa and MasterCard, allow users to charge purchases up to the credit limit of the card. When applying for a standard credit card, the applicant's income, credit history, and other factors are taken into account. Banks may offer different kinds of credit cards, depending on the risk level of the applicant. Gold and platinum cards, for example, usually have a high credit limit and a relatively low interest rate and are offered only to people with a solid financial history. These cards may offer rewards such as points that can be redeemed for airfare or gasoline purchases, but they may also charge a hefty annual fee.

> "Sometimes when you charge too much money on your credit card, you'll have bad credit and you probably won't get approved when you want to buy something."
>
> —Gia, a student

Teenagers with no credit history, and others who have been rejected for a standard credit card, may obtain

A Hip-Hop Visa Card

Entrepreneur Russell Simmons has had a long career as a hip-hop mogul, gay rights activist, television producer, and philanthropist. He also entered the field of personal finance with his own debit card, the RushCard. Created in 2003, the RushCard is a prepaid Visa debit card that can help people establish a good credit history. There are no credit checks when applying for a RushCard, and cardholders pay an initial fee to activate the card. "It's very inexpensive [and] it builds credit," Simmons told *Forbes* magazine in 2011. Monthly charges and other fees also apply, depending on which of two plans is chosen.

The RushCard, however, has not been without its problems. It has come under fire for marketing to teens: anyone thirteen years old or older can get a card (with parental consent for youth under eighteen.) In October 2015 a technical glitch prevented cardholders from accessing their accounts for several days, leaving customers—some of whom used the card for all their financial needs—out of luck.

Other celebrities, most notably the Kardashians, have tried to join the prepaid card arena, but only Russell Simmons has so far shown staying power.

credit with a bank's secured credit card. When a person applies for a secured card, he or she deposits money into an account with the credit card issuer. This is usually equal to or more than the amount of the card's credit limit: for example, if $1,000 is deposited, the card's credit limit could be established at $500 to $1,000. With this type of card, the credit limit is "secured" by the user's money in the account, and the bank assumes no risk. If the cardholder does not pay for what is charged on the card, the bank can take the money directly from the user's account. Unlike debit cards, using a secured card helps build a credit history. Financial adviser Suze Orman, in her book *The Money Book for the Young, Fabulous & Broke*, says, "A secured card can be a first step toward qualifying for a regular credit card."

Many people, for one reason or another, choose not to have a savings or checking account with a bank. If they need credit, they may choose to obtain a prepaid credit card. This type of card is similar to a secured credit card, but in practice it acts more like a debit card. After signing up for a prepaid card, the user adds money to the card up to a predetermined spending limit. When a purchase is made, the amount is deducted from the card's account. When the spending limit is reached, the card is no longer valid unless more money is loaded into the account. Prepaid cards are popular with young people and have been marketed specifically to them by such celebrities as New York Yankees infielder Alex Rodriguez, entrepreneur Russell Simmons, and rapper Lil Wayne. According to a 2015 survey, one-third of the millennial generation has used a prepaid credit card.

Interest, Fees, and Credit Limits

Several factors should be considered before choosing a credit card. One of the most important features of any credit card is the interest rate. This is where the banks make money with cards they issue, and they make it from the cardholders.

When the monthly credit card bill arrives in the mail or online, the cardholder may pay either the entire bill or only a portion of the amount due. If the bill is paid in full, the outstanding account balance returns to zero until

Beware of Hidden Fees

Sometimes the fees that are buried in the fine print of a credit card contract can cause a wealth of problems. Luke had one hundred dollars in his bank account, which came with a debit card. After using his card at the mall and the movies, Luke hit the local gas station. He figured that, after the fill-up, he still had twenty dollars in his account. He was surprised when his next statement showed a fee for spending more money than he had in his account.

Luke soon discovered that the gas station automatically charged a temporary flat fee of fifty dollars when a debit card is used at the pump, later changing it to the actual cost of the gas pumped when the charge is posted. So, although the actual cost of the gas was only twenty-five dollars, the fifty dollar fee put Luke temporarily over his limit. Such fees are listed in the bank account's disclosure statement, so the moral of the story is: read the fine print.

the card is used for another purchase. If the bill is not paid in full, then interest is charged. Interest is a percentage of the remaining balance on the bill and is added each month until the bill is paid off. This is known as revolving credit.

Credit card interest rates can vary widely. In 2016 the average rate was just under 16 percent, with some cards having rates as high as 30 percent. Some cards offer an introductory interest rate of 0 percent as an incentive to sign up for the card. Such rates are temporary, typically lasting from twelve to twenty-one months before the card's higher interest rate kicks in. Zero-interest credit cards can sometimes lead to overspending. In the book *Cash and Credit Information for Teens*, Neal, a sophomore at Southern Illinois University, says, "I try to cut down on what I use, but my one [card] has a zero per-cent interest rate for a year." Before he knew it, Neal had maxed out his card's $3,000 limit.

Another important aspect of a credit card is fees. Some cards charge an annual fee for using the card, often fifteen to thirty-five dollars per year. Cards may charge a fee for late payments, transferring a balance from another card, getting a cash advance, going over the credit limit, and even for closing the account. Every card has its own set of fees, which is why it is important to shop around before deciding on which credit card to apply for. Prepaid cards are especially notorious for the many fees they charge, including an activation fee, a monthly maintenance fee, a charge for paper state-ments, and a fee for ATM transactions.

The card's credit limit is also an important feature. The maximum that can be charged on a card is specified when the card is applied for, and the amount depends on the credit history of the applicant. Credit limits can range from about $1,000 to many thousands of dollars. Often banks raise a low limit after the cardholder estab-lishes a history of on-time payments. Once a cardhold-er's purchases reach the credit limit, further attempts at using the card will result in a purchase being declined, an embarrassing situation at the checkout counter. Al-ternately, the purchase may be accepted, but a stiff fee will be added to the account by the issuer.

The Dangers of Credit Cards

People do not often think that the credit card in their wallet or purse can be dangerous; obviously, they can-not really do physical harm to their owners. But there are financial dangers lurking in those little plastic cards.

Because of the ease of using plastic for purchases, spending can get quickly out of hand. It takes willpower, and a sensible budget, to keep from overspending. Studies have shown that people spend more when using a credit or debit card than when they use cash. As a student named Gia says in *Not Your Parents' Money Book*, "Sometimes when you charge too much money on your credit card, you'll have bad credit and you probably won't get approved when you want to buy something."

Lost or stolen cards present another danger. A thief can rack up numerous charges on a stolen card before the cardholder even knows it is missing. Cardholders are generally liable for only fifty dollars of unauthorized purchases made on a stolen card, if the issuer is notified of the loss in a timely manner. Credit card fraud, part of a larger problem known as identity theft, can escalate to the point where a person's financial life is ruined.

Credit card numbers, and not just the physical card itself, can also be stolen. An unscrupulous store clerk can write down a customer's card number and use it for online purchases. This happened in 2008 when a Pizza Hut employee went on a shopping spree using a customer's credit card number. The employee spent $6,700 before being caught. Although under the law the cardholder is not liable for losses when only the account number is stolen, it can create an anxious situation nonetheless.

Chapter Three

Loans

Credit cards are generally safe and convenient for making everyday purchases. A responsible person will only charge as much as he or she can afford to pay back when the bill arrives. But sometimes unanticipated expenses can wreak havoc with the best family budget: an accident that totals the family car, an illness requiring a lengthy hospital stay, or a furnace that dies in the middle of winter. Other life situations, such as the purchase of a car or house, are usually too costly to pay for in full. In these or other similar circumstances, taking out a loan may be the only practical way to handle such large or unexpected expenses.

Types of Loans

Although teenagers do not have to worry about a large purchase such as a house until later in life, there are situations where a loan may be beneficial. For many teenagers, that situation is applying for college. Having a bachelor's degree can mean an additional $1 million in lifetime earnings over someone with only a high school

Young car buyers discuss details of a loan offered by a car dealership. A car is often the first major purchase for a teenager—and the financial responsibility of owning a car can be an eye-opening experience.

diploma. But those extra earnings can come with a hefty price tag. According to the College Board, a non-profit organization that administers standardized tests and provides information about college admissions, in 2015 the average tuition for a four-year public college was about $9,400 per year; for private colleges, annual tuition averaged more than $32,000.

Scholarships and grants can help with the cost of college, but not all students will qualify for them. For these students, loans can make an education possible. Studies have shown that about 70 percent of college students have taken out loans for their education. Kevin, a college graduate in Alexandria, Virginia, decided that his college education was worth taking out loans. On the website Student Debt Crisis, Kevin says, "I borrowed the majority of my college costs believing that I was investing in my future. No one made me borrow the money. No one coerced me into going to college. A college degree was something that I decided, on my own, was important to me."

Buying a car is often a teenager's first major purchase. Automobile loans can finance the purchase of a new or used car, and can be the first opportunity to build a good credit history. An auto loan usually requires a down payment, with monthly payments on the balance lasting from four to seven years. The expense of owning a car may be an eye-opening experience for a teen. State laws usually require a minimum level of liability insurance on a car, which will be an extra expense in addition to the loan payment. Gas, maintenance, and unexpected repairs also add to the cost.

A home is the largest and most important purchase that most people will make in their lifetime. But very few have enough money to buy a house or condominium outright. A mortgage is a loan taken out to allow the purchase of a home with a small down payment and then financing, or mortgaging, the balance with interest over a number of years. Home mortgages can last anywhere from ten to thirty years or more. Once a home is purchased, some people also obtain loans from department or furniture stores to furnish the new residence.

Loans can either be secured or unsecured. In a secured loan, the amount borrowed is backed up by something of value that the borrower owns; this is called

> "I borrowed the majority of my college costs believing that I was investing in my future. No one made me borrow the money. No one coerced me into going to college. A college degree was something that I decided, on my own, was important to me."
>
> —Kevin, a college student

25

collateral. A house, car, or other valuable item can be used as collateral. If the loan is not repaid, the collateral can be sold to recover the lender's money. Where collateral is not available, an unsecured loan may be issued to the borrower. People with poor credit may apply for an unsecured loan. With nothing of value to back it up but the borrower's ability to pay it back, the unsecured loan is usually issued for smaller amounts than a secured loan and has a shorter payback period and a much higher interest rate.

Where to Get a Loan

As with credit cards, most people turn to their bank when seeking a loan. The money that people deposit in their savings or checking accounts does not just sit around gathering dust inside the bank's vault. The bank puts the money to work, loaning it to people who want to buy cars or houses, or for any number of other reasons. People who wish to start a business, as well as established businesses that need new equipment or desire to expand their operations, may also turn to a bank for a loan.

Most banks have employees called loan officers whose job it is to evaluate applications and authorize loans for those people or businesses who are deemed good financial risks. Banks will subjectively assess an applicant's character and look at his or her credit history, record of on-time payments of such debts as credit card purchases, and available collateral. Like banks, credit unions also issue loans, as long as the loan applicant is a member of the credit union. As they are nonprofit organizations working for the good of their members, loan interest rates at credit unions may be lower than those assessed by a bank.

For teenagers looking to attend college, the federal government has several loan programs for the prospective student and his or her parents. The US Department of Education offers direct subsidized or unsubsidized loans, sometimes referred to as Stafford Loans. Subsidized loans are available for students with financial need, and the government will pay the interest while a student is in school and six months after graduation. Students with no financial need but a desire to finance their college education can apply for an unsubsidized loan; the student must pay interest on these loans during the college

Loans for Young Farmers

For youth living in rural areas who are members of 4-H or Future Farmers of America, the Farm Service Agency of the US Department of Agriculture offers loans to help youth get a start in farming. Rural youth loans of up to $5,000 are available for youth from ten to twenty years of age who create income-producing projects that will generate enough profit to repay the loan. Interest rates are low, and the term of the loans ranges from one to seven years. Rural youth loans can be used to purchase livestock, seeds, farm equipment, and other agricultural items.

Blaine, a thirteen-year-old in Ohio, used his loan to purchase cows, beginning with a pair of Herefords and, with further loans, ultimately increasing his herd to twelve. He is proud of the fact that he has made a profit and repaid the loans. A rural youth loan "teaches kids so many skills, including money management," says Lisa Kinsey, a loan officer in New Philadelphia, Ohio. It also helps groom the next generation of farmers who will feed the United States and the world.

years. A Perkins Loan, also available for students with financial need, is issued by the college or university and is subsidized by the government. It has a 5 percent interest rate, and repayment is deferred as long as the student carries at least a half-time load at the school. Parents may apply for a Federal Direct PLUS Loan for their dependent undergraduate son or daughter, regardless of financial need.

At a time when just about anything can be found on the Internet, it is not surprising that the web is also a source for loans. Several online companies offer personal loans or home mortgages, either through their own financing or by acting as a broker for numerous lending institutions. Care must be taken, however, as some lending sites will sell personal information to other online companies, resulting in damage to a borrower's credit history and a barrage of unwanted telephone calls and e-mails soliciting business.

Understanding Interest

When taking out a loan, the borrower should understand what interest is and how it works. Banks and credit unions charge interest on the loans they issue; it is how they make a profit from allowing people to use the money their customers have deposited with them. Looking at it from the borrower's perspective, paying interest is the cost of using other people's money.

Interest is a percentage of the amount of the loan and is usually expressed as the annual percentage rate (APR). The APR will vary depending on the type of financing sought (personal or car loan, small business loan, or home mortgage), the borrower's credit history, and whether the interest is fixed or variable. A fixed

Tips for College Loans

In 1971 the tuition for a year at Harvard University was $2,600. In the fall of 2016, freshmen at the prestigious school paid more than $47,000—a 1,700 percent increase. The cost of college in general has been rising at an alarming rate: from 2003 to 2013, tuition grew by nearly 80 percent. Many students would be unable to go to college without taking out a loan. Although student loans can be confusing, a few tips will help make the choice easier.

1. Shopping for loans and comparing interest rates can help save money in the long run.
2. Know how much tuition costs, but remember to include other expenses such as room and board, fees, and textbooks.
3. Borrow only as much as is needed, which may be less than the total amount offered.
4. Reading and understanding the loan agreement—including the fine print—will eliminate unwelcome surprises when it comes time to repay the loan.
5. Making interest-only payments while still in college will help lower the total repayment figure after graduation.
6. Contact the college's financial aid office if any part of the loan process is unclear.

interest rate remains the same for the duration of the loan whereas a variable interest rate may go up or down over time. A typical interest rate on a car loan might be anywhere from 1 to 5 percent or more, depending on the length of the loan and other factors. Over the past fifty years, home mortgage interest rates have varied from more than 16 percent to 3 or 4 percent over the typical mortgage length of fifteen or thirty years. Many economic factors affect the mortgage interest rate, including location of the property, length of the mortgage, the strength of the nation's economy, and the specific provisions of the loan.

The concept of interest may be difficult for teens, and even for some adults, to fully understand. But some parents make the idea of borrowing with interest a reality for their kids. A father in Fort Collins, Colorado, loaned his son, Calvin, twenty dollars at 5 percent interest per week. After paying eight dollars on the loan over a few weeks, Calvin gave his dad twelve dollars to repay the balance. He was surprised to learn that, because of the interest, he still owed his father five dollars and twenty-five cents. Calvin learned his lesson about interest well: he paid his father back and then began loaning money to his friends—with interest.

Economics classes in school may teach general information about loans and interest, but there are other ways to learn as well. A visit to a local bank or credit union can provide a potential borrower with literature on loans and interest as well as other aspects of personal finance. The local public library and websites such as MyMoney.gov can also be a great source of financial information.

Paying Off Loans

The one undeniable truth about loans is that sooner or later they must be repaid. How, and how promptly, a loan is paid back can make a difference in terms of interest paid and a good credit history. There are two parts of a loan: the principal and the interest. The principal is the amount for which the loan was taken out, and the interest is the cost to the borrower of using the loaned money.

When a monthly payment is made, it is usually applied to the loan in a specific way. If there are any outstanding fees on the loan, they are paid first. Then the interest that has accrued for that month is paid. Finally, the remaining part of the payment is applied to reducing the principal. Making regular monthly payments will pay off the loan in the amount of time specified when the loan was initiated—perhaps thirty years for a home mortgage or five years for an auto loan.

> "It's funny how you can do all of the right things—go to college, get a job— and one day wake up with crushing debt."
>
> —Stephanie, a college graduate

Even loans that may seem overwhelming can be paid off using perseverance and ingenuity. As twenty-six-year-old Stephanie tells the *Forbes* website, "It's funny how you can do all of the right things—go to college, get a job—and one day wake up with crushing debt." Stephanie's debt was indeed crushing: $90,000 in student loans and credit card charges. But by getting extra jobs, taking in a roommate, and canceling her gym membership, Stephanie was able to put an extra $2,000 a month toward her debt. "Paying down my debt," she says, "has changed the way that I see my money."

When used sparingly and paid off promptly, loans can be an effective way to get through some of life's hard times. But relying too much on loans can quickly turn life into a quagmire of debt that may be difficult to escape.

Chapter Four

Too Much Debt

Americans are among the most prosperous people in the world, with an average net worth of more than $350,000 per adult. But Americans also are near the top in another financial category: debt. In 2016 the average household debt for people who carried a balance on their credit cards was $15,863, for a whopping national total of $940 billion. How did Americans get themselves into such debt? For past generations, the idea of living within one's means was the key to financial security. Simply put, this means that a person did not spend more than the income he or she brought home. Food, shelter, and clothing for the family came first, and any money left over after these were secured could be used for the purchase of nonessential items. Although credit was available, going into debt was often frowned upon.

Today living within one's means is still the best way to avoid financial problems. But it seems to be getting harder to live a life without credit. The stigma of buying on credit has largely disappeared, and offers for credit cards show up in the mail with alarming frequency. It takes willpower to pass up the latest extravagance when it is so easy to just hand over a credit card and take your purchase home. But that is exactly how people can get into too much debt: letting their desires override their self-discipline. And when that happens, financial ruin can be the result.

When Debt Grows

College student David found it easy to get a credit card. He used it to buy small stuff—tickets to sporting events, concerts, and fast-food restaurant meals. After maxing out his first card, he got another, and then more cards, paying just the minimum amount on each one. Before he knew it, David's small purchases had helped get him $30,000 in debt. When David's parents discovered their son's debt, they threatened to take control of his finances. "Not only was this humiliating," David reveals in a post on the website On Your Own, "but it was a severe wake-up call, and to this day I'm grateful for it. . . . I cut out fast food and trips to the convenience store. Eliminating those alone saved me over $100 every month."

David ultimately realized that his reckless spending had gotten him into too much debt, and he was able to climb out of the financial hole he had created. But not everyone who incurs massive amounts of debt does so out of a simple lack of willpower. Many people are forced into debt due to circumstances beyond their control. Losing a job or being forced to take a pay cut,

> "I pay as much as I can every month but [my debt] never seems to go away. It seems that every time I think I am getting things under control something else pops up like a car repair or another unexpected expense."
>
> —Mark, an unemployed worker

33

Gambling: A Loser's Game

One of the worst ways to get into debt is gambling. Yet for some people it can become an addiction. The International Centre for Youth Gambling Problems and High-Risk Behaviours in Montreal, Canada, reports that up to 80 percent of high school students have gambled during the most recent school year. Of those students, 4 to 6 percent can be classified as being addicted to gambling. Symptoms of pathological gambling include enjoying the rush from gambling, betting more money even when losing, and always hoping for the elusive "big score." As one eighteen-year-old put it, "When I lose, it's really good because I am on [a] mission. . . . I have something to do . . . try to win my money back."

Besides the loss of hard-earned money, other consequences of gambling are anxiety; changes in personal relations; and problems in school, including increased absences and poor grades. These consequences can have a profound effect on a teenager's future. School counselors, support groups, and free hotline services are available for teens with a gambling addiction. Early intervention can prevent a lifetime of anxiety and costly problems.

reduced hours at work, an unexpected illness or accident, or other unforeseen circumstances may leave a person no choice but to rely on credit. On the blog *I Will Teach You to Be Rich*, Mark says he went into debt "trying to keep myself 'afloat' during a lengthy unemployment. I pay as much as I can every month but it never seems to go away. It seems that every time I think I am getting things under control something else pops up like a car repair or another unexpected expense."

Despite the Affordable Care Act, commonly known

as Obamacare, signed into law in 2010, health care is still one of the largest expenses many people will face. As the costs of surgical procedures, hospital stays, prescription drugs, and doctor visits continue to rise, more people are forced to go into debt. In fact, medical expenses are the number one source of debt in the United States. Elizabeth and Britt's son Orin was born in 2013 with a heart condition. Britt's insurance from work covered about half the medical expenses. But soon, as a cost-cutting measure, his company eliminated insurance for its employees. Orin's medical bills continued to pile up. "I've sold furniture out of my own house to try to pay off some of the bills," Elizabeth tells *USA Today*.

There are many other ways that debt may accumulate. Poor money management, undertaking risky activities like gambling, or simply being unaware of such financial basics as how to balance a checkbook or understanding interest rates on credit cards and loans can all result in too much debt. Signs that point to the overuse of credit include buying necessities like food with credit cards, using one credit card to pay off another, and borrowing money from friends or family to make debt payments. If these signs are ignored, debt can quickly turn into a major problem.

The Consequences of Too Much Debt

The old phrase *too much of a good thing* means that overdoing a pleasurable activity, like indulging in chocolate or scarfing down a pizza, can actually have an undesirable effect, such as weight gain. But too much of a bad thing—such as overwhelming debt—can literally ruin a person's life. Horror stories about the consequences of getting too far into debt are all too common. Tyler worked

A shopper tries out a sale-priced tablet. The ease of using credit cards to pay for a new tablet or phone, dinners with friends, tickets to a baseball game, and other enjoyable pursuits can quickly lead to a mountain of debt.

full-time while in college, but his paychecks could not keep up with his extravagant spending habits. He used credit cards to buy new desktop and laptop computers and a Mustang that he modified at an even greater cost. Tyler was spending far more than his $35,000 annual salary, and soon his credit problems began to catch up with him. His car was stolen, so he bought another Mustang. A hospital bill drove him further into debt. When he had to return the Mustang because he could not make the payments, Tyler knew he had hit rock bottom.

For many young adults, the most common tales of too much debt center around student loans. In 2016 student debt topped $1.2 trillion, with about 43 million Americans having taken out loans for their college education. This debt continues to rise, leading to horror stories about overburdened graduates struggling to pay back their loans. Just a year after her college graduation, Charice had $30,000 in debt and could not find a job. Another graduate, Artie, studied to be an architect, but with over $200,000 in student loans, he had to work two jobs that were not in his chosen field to make the payments. After making monthly payments of more than $350 for fourteen years, social worker Mary still owed $25,000 on her student loan. The Internet is filled with similar stories of people who hoped that a college degree would improve their lives but never realized the price they would be paying.

As Mary learned, going into too much debt can have unexpected long-term consequences—and not just bills that will not go away. With too many outstanding debts or a record of late payments, a person may not be able to get a loan or a new credit card. A new car may be financially out of reach, making

> "I've sold furniture out of my own house to try to pay off some of the bills,"
>
> —Elizabeth, parent of a boy born with a heart condition

an older used car the only option; a fast-food meal may have to substitute for an evening at a nice restaurant.

Psychologists have confirmed the connection between debt and stress. According to the *Atlantic* magazine, a 2013 study revealed that people with significant financial problems "perceived more stress, had more symptoms of depression, anxiety, and ill-health."

Excessive debt can lead to low self-esteem, severe depression, loss of sleep, and even suicide. The fear that a collection agency is calling every time the phone rings can adversely affect the quality of life.

Is Getting into Debt Too Easy?

One of the biggest factors linked to the dangers of excessive debt is that credit is generally so easy to get. There are many unscrupulous enterprises that will offer credit to anyone, even people who have a poor credit history and may already be deep in debt. Such practices are called predatory lending because the lenders prey on the elderly, minorities, and the poor who have little or no means of getting credit any other way.

Tonya had fallen behind on her rent and was hit with unexpected emergency hospital bills. With no other source of funds, she took out a short-term loan to pay her rent and utilities. Called a payday loan, it required Tonya to pay it back when she got her next paycheck. But her check was not enough, so she took out another payday loan to cover the first. Eventually she had seven payday loans, with annual interest rates up to 500 percent—which translates to a significant amount of money being added onto her loans.

At just about any time of day television commercials tout easy credit through payday and other short-term loans. While the lenders emphasize the convenience and ease of obtaining such loans, they rely on the borrower's inability to pay them back—adding more interest and late fees to the borrowed amount. Expensive short-term loans include automobile title loans. With this type of loan, the lender holds the title to the borrower's car as collateral. The typical term of an auto title loan is fifteen

Misunderstanding Debt

Teenagers can be very knowledgeable about subjects they are interested in, but when it comes to finances, many have misconceptions about money and debt. According to the Personal Finance Education Group (PFEG), many teenagers are developing a "worryingly laidback" attitude toward debt.

Part of this problem stems from teens' poor understanding of basic financial concepts. For example, a survey showed that almost 25 percent of youth aged fourteen to eighteen thought an overdraft on a bank account meant they could spend more than they earned rather than indicating they had spent more than what was in their account. One in twenty teens believed that they did not have to pay back credit card debt. Some college graduates think they will make enough at their first job to easily pay back their student loans, which is usually not the case. Others believe that declaring bankruptcy will wipe out their student loans (it will not).

In the British newspaper the *Telegraph*, PFEG chief executive Wendy van den Hende says that teenagers "appear to be drifting toward an adulthood of debt." Better financial education, from schools and parents, is needed to keep teens from a dire financial future.

to thirty days. If the borrower defaults, his car can be repossessed and sold to pay off the debt. Annual interest rates on these loans can reach 100 percent or higher, and various fees can raise the cost even further.

With thousands of outlets nationwide and millions of dollars in annual sales, rent-to-own stores make it easy to get nearly anything for the home. By offering appealing payment plans that end with the purchaser owning the item, these stores seem to be an ideal place for people with poor credit histories to get the things they want. But a hard look at the numbers reveals the true cost of such easy credit. The *Consumer Reports* website reveals that a Toshiba laptop was being offered from a rent-to-own store at $38.99 a week for forty-eight weeks. The total of the payments worked out to be $1,872—for a computer with a retail price of $612. It is equivalent of an interest rate of 311 percent, much higher than even the highest credit card rate. Some rent-to-own stores offer the customer the option of purchasing the rented item before the contract ends, but the price is usually more than what standard retail stores charge for the same item. Postponing such a purchase and saving up for the item is a much better financial practice. In the case of the laptop, weekly depositing $38.99 in a savings account instead of paying a rental company would take only sixteen weeks to save enough to purchase the computer, a savings of over $1,200.

For all its convenience and usefulness, credit can quickly get out of hand if it is not used intelligently and carefully monitored. Fortunately, for those who are drowning in debt, there are ways to resolve the situation if they are willing to make sacrifices and change their financial habits.

Chapter Five

Digging Out of Debt

Most of the problems that get people into too much debt could be eliminated by following a simple rule: do not charge more than you can afford to pay when the bill comes due. In reality, that sentiment is easier said than done. Many people have gotten so deep into debt that they feel the future looks hopeless. A 2014 survey revealed that almost one in five Americans who are already in debt believe they will never pay off their debts in their lifetime. But getting out of debt is possible, even for those who are overwhelmed by mounting expenses and unpaid bills. The steps to undo years of poor financial decisions may not be easy, but they are a necessary part of bringing personal finances under control.

Assessing the Damage

Some people do not realize how serious their debt problems are. Rachel, a single mother of three, had no idea that financial disaster was threatening her family's well-being. "I was just trying to keep up with everybody else," she says in a *Money* magazine online article. "I was always spending extra on Christmas and on birthdays.

Curbing Impulse Buying

"I have a bad habit I have to admit to," says Arlene on the *Huffington Post* website. "I am an impulse buyer. Often, I will buy something that I don't need, put it away, and the next time I see the item I think: 'Now exactly why did I buy that?'"

Impulse buying can quickly wreck a budget. To avoid impulse buying, experts recommend staying away from places where the enticement to buy unnecessary items can be strong. Coming home from the mall with an armload of impulse buys can be exciting, but it will lead to remorse once the bills arrive. Shopping with a friend can help prevent impulse buying; the hope is that a friend would be more objective, which could help prevent an emotional purchase. When shopping for food, experts also suggest, never go to the grocery store on an empty stomach, a condition that tends to make everything on the shelves look delicious.

For people who feel that their impulse spending is a disease similar to alcoholism, Debtors Anonymous provides hope and support. At local meetings, people share their stories of overspending and provide encouragement and support for others who are at risk.

. . . I wasn't aware of how much debt I was in." In fact, Rachel's debt was a staggering $179,625.

The first step in digging out of debt is to determine how bad the situation is. Make a list of all financial liabilities: credit card balances; mortgages and home equity loans; auto, furniture, and other consumer loans; student loans; and any other outstanding debts. This can be done with a simple pencil and paper or with a more comprehensive spreadsheet program such as Microsoft Excel. There are also many free online tools that can help determine debt. Comparing the amount of outstanding debt with household income will give a clear, sometimes shocking, picture of the financial situation.

The services of a credit counselor can often be valuable in sorting out a complicated debt situation, where years of bills piling up are almost impossible to make sense of. "A disturbing number of people come to our offices with grocery bags filled with bills," reports credit counselor Gail Cunningham in *Money* magazine. Credit counselors are trained to examine a person's credit history, outstanding debt, and income and propose solutions for getting out of debt and avoiding future financial problems.

Repairing the Damage

Once a person understands his or her financial condition, repairing the damage can begin. The first step should be to stop all unnecessary spending. This may sound simple, but it takes a strong dose of willpower for it to succeed. Jasmine, a high school student, saw a new video game that she really wanted and began saving up for it. But before long her resolve began to falter, and soon she had spent all the money she had saved on other things. Jasmine's desire to spend got the best of her willpower.

To resist the temptation of unnecessary spending, credit cards should be cut up or at least put in a place where they will be inconvenient to access. Cutting back on everyday spending can also help. Buying store brand groceries instead of name brands will save cash, usually without any noticeable loss in quality. Bringing a homemade lunch to school or work will save a surprising amount of money over hitting fast-food restaurants. Home-brewed coffee can be just as satisfying as a coffee shop's frothy, five-dollar concoction.

There are many useful strategies for repaying loans. Most financial advisers recommend paying off the debts with the highest interest rate first. "The best move from a purely financial perspective is to attack the highest-interest rate cards first," says financial planner Scott Halliwell on the *U.S. News & World Report* website. Attacking the high-rate bills first will lower the total interest that must be paid. Another method is to create what is called a debt snowball. With this strategy, the minimum payment is made on all bills except the one with the smallest outstanding balance. As much money as possible is then put toward eliminating that bill. Once it is paid off, the next-lowest bill is targeted, and so on, creating a snowball effect as debts are paid off one after another. A psychological reward is a major benefit of this method. "For people that need to see instant results to keep them motivated, that may be the best process for them, because it's the quickest way to get them to a successful conclusion," says financial expert Bruce McClary on the Bankrate website.

> "I was just trying to keep up with everybody else. I was always spending extra on Christmas and on birthdays. . . . I wasn't aware of how much debt I was in."
>
> —Rachel, a single mother

Debt management programs are offered by many nonprofit organizations that are regulated by the Federal Trade Commission. These programs will arrange a payment plan in which the person makes monthly deposits into an account and the money is then used to pay credit card bills, student loans, and other debts. Many creditors will charge a lower interest rate for anyone repaying a loan through a debt management program.

Employing some simple strategies can also help with digging out of the debt hole. Finding a second job, renting out a room in your house, canceling expensive utilities such as cable television or a landline phone, and selling possessions that do not get much use are all ways to gain extra cash that can be put toward bills. Negotiating with creditors can also help reduce debt. A call to a credit card company to explain financial difficulties could lead to lower interest rates or waived fees. Regularly reviewing bills may reveal costly mistakes. Stores will issue refunds for overcharges due to incorrectly marked items or checkout scanning errors. Hospital billing errors are common and can be negotiated if a careful examination of bills and insurance filings uncovers a mistake. Professionals called medical billing advocates help patients find and correct such errors.

Handling Debt Collectors

When a bill is long overdue and efforts to get the debtor to pay fail to resolve the situation, creditors can hire a collection agency to act on their behalf. Collection agencies specialize in debt recovery. They contact the debtor by phone and try to make arrangements for repayment of the outstanding balance. Many agencies work on commission, receiving a percentage of the debt recovered. Although the collection industry is regulated by both state and federal laws, agencies sometimes use questionable or even illegal tactics to persuade debtors to pay.

Collection calls may come at all hours of the day or night. Scare tactics such as personal threats, verbal abuse, imitating a law enforcement officer, and stalking a person's Facebook account are often employed. One unscrupulous agency even set up an office to look like a courtroom, complete with a fake judge, and held phony proceedings to intimidate debtors into paying. Not all collectors use these extreme tactics, but even a polite call to request payment of an overdue bill can create anxiety.

Sometimes an agency will try to collect a debt from the wrong person due to faulty information, identity theft, or a misunderstanding. When seventeen-year-old Heather got a new cell phone in 2014, she began receiving automated debt collection calls. Within months she had gotten more than two hundred of these so-called robo-calls, sometimes even during class. The real issue was that Heather had no debt: the calls were for a different person.

Collecting from the Collectors

Small-town West Virginia mom Diana received a call from an unscrupulous bill collector who threatened to begin legal proceedings to take her house if she did not pay off a loan—a debt she told him she did not owe. She soon began receiving threatening calls that used vulgar language and promised physical harm. Frightened but undeterred, Diana turned the tables and began her own lawsuit, charging the collector with harassment and illegal collection practices.

It took Diana a year to find a lawyer who would take her case, but her persistence paid off. A judge awarded her $10,086,000 in damages, the largest judgment ever against a collection agency. The story of Diana's lawsuit was broadcast on the ABC News program *Nightline*. Ultimately, the Federal Trade Commission shut down the agency and its affiliated offices. Although Diana will probably never collect the over $10 million, she is glad to have brought the problem to the public's attention. As she told ABC News, "I hope that it sends a message to other debt collectors out there that you have to follow the law."

When she finally was able to talk to a live person, the calls stopped—for a while. They soon resumed, and Heather's family began a lawsuit against the collection agency.

The best way to avoid debt collectors, of course, is to make sure that outstanding debts are paid promptly. Keeping track of bills and due dates will help eliminate missed payments, and canceled checks or credit card records will provide proof of on-time payments. If a collection agency does make contact by phone or texts, debtors have certain rights. Collection agencies cannot use obscenity, make threats of arrest or property seizure, or contact a third party—a relative or coworker—with your financial information. Negotiating with an agency may result in a lower payment, especially if it will accept a reasonable lump-sum reimbursement.

Bankruptcy—the Last Resort

When debts become so overwhelming that there is little or no chance of the creditors ever being paid back, bankruptcy may be the only solution. By the time Amanda was a senior in college, her irresponsible spending had nearly maxed out four credit cards. At the age of twenty-three, out of college with a low-paying job and living at home, Amanda filed for bankruptcy. Although much of her debt was resolved, she still had student loans to pay and could not get a new credit card for seven years.

Bankruptcy is a federal court procedure that was established in the US Constitution. A special court, the US Bankruptcy Court, is charged with resolving bankruptcy cases, which begin when a debtor files a voluntary petition of bankruptcy. There are generally two types, or chapters, of bankruptcy proceedings for individuals. The most common type of bankruptcy is Chapter

7, in which property is surrendered to a court-appointed trustee. The trustee sells the property and gives the proceeds to the creditors, thus settling the debt. Property essential for living (cars, household goods, and clothing) are exempt from being surrendered, although items not deemed indispensable, such as a second car, a valuable coin collection, or cash, can be taken. Although most debts are discharged by a Chapter 7 bankruptcy, student loans are not and must still be repaid. Chapter 13 bankruptcy is a financial reorganization option that allows the debtor to keep his or her property. A payment plan is then created that reimburses the creditors within three to five years. When either a Chapter 7 or Chapter 13 bankruptcy is filed with the court, all collection attempts and legal actions initiated by the creditors are halted.

> "Do everything you can to dig out of a big debt hole."
>
> —*Financial adviser Suze Orman*

Many law firms deal exclusively with bankruptcies, and they make filing a relatively simple process for a hefty upfront fee. But bankruptcy should not be a first option. Although it provides immediate help for overwhelmed debtors, it has serious consequences that affect a person's financial future. With a bankruptcy on record, credit will be more costly. Interest rates on the purchase of a car or house will be significantly higher or the loan may be declined outright. Bankruptcy also takes an emotional toll, triggering feelings of embarrassment, guilt, and shame. In her book *The Money Book for the Young, Fabulous & Broke*, financial adviser Suze Orman recommends, "Do everything you can to dig out of a big debt hole." It will take time, and it may require many personal sacrifices, but getting out of debt is the only way to assure a financially solid future.

Chapter Six

Assessing Your Financial Health

Just as doctors recommend regular checkups to ensure a healthy body, money experts suggest a regular evaluation of personal finances to make sure that spending is under control, debt is manageable, and financial goals are being met. There are many aspects that should be taken into account when assessing a personal financial program.

The most important tool is the budget. A monthly evaluation of a personal budget will reveal where the money goes and should uncover any problems. For example, the consistent use of credit cards to cover a budget shortfall is a danger sign that something needs to be corrected, either by bringing in more income or limiting spending. Besides listing necessary expenses, a good budget will also have a category for regular savings, which will build up a reserve of money so that future purchases will not have to be bought on credit. "It's about goals," says financial expert Andrew Housser in *The Complete Guide to Personal Finance for Teenagers and College Students*. "It's hard to get somewhere if you don't know where you're going. . . . Once you have goals in mind, you can budget for those goals and adjust accordingly."

Keeping track of credit card spending can be as easy as creating a file for monthly credit card bills. Examining the bill when it arrives can reveal good or poor credit management. If an assessment shows that necessities are being charged, or that there are too many impulse items on the bill, changes in spending habits are probably in order. Many credit card companies provide a year-end summary of spending, either sent with the final bill or available online. The summary is divided into various spending categories such as groceries, automotive, entertainment, and restaurants. Reviewing this summary can help create awareness of the extent of credit use and perhaps encourage a change in spending habits.

Smart Spending Habits

Everyone likes to go shopping for the latest fashions or electronic gadgets, and no one enjoys a spending spree more than teenagers. An afternoon at the mall with friends can be fun and exciting, but it can also be dangerous for a well-planned budget. Developing smart spending habits can make shopping more enjoyable and can also help teens avoid getting into financial trouble that can create problems in the future.

Almost all purchases fall into two categories—wants or needs—and the smart teen shopper will learn the difference. The primary human needs are food, clothing, and shelter. Other needs can include transportation to

Concertgoers enjoy a night of live music. Learning to stay within a budget means balancing spending between wants (like concerts) and needs (like food and rent).

school or work; personal items such as prescriptions, glasses, or contact lenses; and school books and supplies. After these basic needs are met, everything else is a want. Concert tickets, a shiny new car, or a ski trip with friends may be enticing, but they are wants rather than needs. Even needs can turn into wants. Everyone must eat, of course, but simple foods prepared at home nourish just as well as (and maybe better than) pricey restaurant meals. A good winter coat is a need in many parts of the country, but an upscale ski jacket with a high-end label is a want. Saving up for the wants in a person's life is the smart way to afford them without resorting to credit and possibly wrecking a budget.

Emotions play a large part in spending money for unnecessary things. Depression, anxiety, unhappiness, or even the stress of a bad hair day can all be triggers for impulse spending. In *Cash and Credit Information for Teens*, Chris Labyk, a former health educator at Southern Illinois University, says, "Some people spend money when they get bored or are depressed, but it is a temporary feeling." Instead of buying something during an emotional time, taking a walk, meeting with a friend, or hitting the gym are all good alternatives to emotional spending.

> "It's an exciting, and also somewhat frightening, time when you begin taking control of your own finances."
>
> —Amy, a high school student

Other smart spending habits include making a shopping list and sticking to it, shopping at outlet stores instead of retail shops, comparison shopping for the best price on big-ticket items, paying cash whenever possible, and bartering for goods or services rather than paying for them. All these strategies will help keep a budget healthy and maintain a good credit rating.

The Importance of Credit Scores

The major factor that determines whether a person will get a loan at a low interest rate, or be approved for a loan at all, rests on one simple three-digit number—the applicant's credit score. The credit score is also known as the FICO score, from the Fair Isaac Company, the firm that originated the formula. It is a measure of the likelihood that a borrower will be able to pay back a loan regularly and on time. Scores range from 300 to 850; the higher the score, the lower the interest rates on loans and credit cards will be.

There are five elements of the credit score that lenders use to determine whether or not to offer a borrower credit. Each element is weighted as a percent of the total:

1. Payment history—35 percent
2. Amounts owed—30 percent
3. Length of credit history—15 percent
4. New credit—10 percent
5. Credit type mix—10 percent

The most important factor is the history of paying past debts. Lenders want to know if their money will be repaid promptly. The amount of money owed on various credit cards and other loans is next in importance. Too much outstanding credit may indicate a danger of being

There's an App for That

With all the remarkable things that a smartphone can do, one of the most useful is budgeting. There are a number of financial planning apps for both iPhone and Android devices that can make budgeting, if not a pleasure, at least more easily manageable.

Mint and PocketGuard are two popular budget apps that let users set up spending categories and goals and then track expenses. They connect to a bank account to access financial information and make transactions. You Need a Budget, a similar app, assigns a job to every dollar in the budget. In ancient (pre-app) times, people often categorized their expenses by placing cash for food, rent, and other items in different envelopes. This system comes into the twenty-first century with GoodBudget and Mvelopes. These apps store money in virtual envelopes and help the user stay on track with both regular and unexpected expenses.

With these apps, and many more that can be found in the App Store and Google Play, managing money is easier than ever. And the best news for your budget is that most of them are free.

financially overextended. A longer length of credit history may mean a higher credit score. People with numerous newer credit accounts may mean a higher risk for the lender, and the type of debt—credit cards, loans, a mortgage—is also taken into account.

A person with a FICO score of 720 or above indicates that he or she would be a good risk for a new loan. At the other end of the scale, a score under 620 means that a loan, if offered, would carry a much higher interest rate to offset the greater risk. Credit scores are based on information generated by three credit-reporting agencies: Experian, Equifax, and TransUnion. These agencies collect debt information and create a credit file for each consumer who has a loan, credit card, or other form of debt. It is from this information that the FICO scores are generated. The scores from each agency may differ slightly since the data examined can vary from agency to agency.

By law, individuals are entitled to receive a free copy of their credit file from the agencies once a year. It is a good idea to review these files annually and report any incorrect information that could negatively affect the credit score. Other ways to improve credit scores are having credit cards with high credit limits but low outstanding balances, not opening too many new accounts at once, and always paying bills on time.

The Global Economy

Walking down the aisles of a modern American store is almost like a lesson in international economics. A quick check of clothing labels will reveal such varied countries of origin as China, Vietnam, Honduras, Pakistan, and many other foreign nations. Even items labeled *Made in the USA* can be manufactured from materials produced

Living on a Budget

High school student Christina has learned how important making a budget is for teenagers. After starting a job and receiving three paychecks, she has begun to put away 60 percent of her income to help pay for future expenses: a car and a college education at a major university. Although her parents require her to save the 60 percent, Christina plans on saving at least some of the remaining 40 percent.

Her parents cover basic living expenses, but Christina has resolved to make good purchasing decisions so that her remaining income will go as far as possible. In the two and a half years she has until entering college, she plans to save $6,000 toward her goals. Christina knows that smart planning and dedication are the key to financial success. As she relates in *The Complete Guide to Personal Finance for Teenagers and College Students*, "In order to be where I want to be in the future, I need to stick to the plan now. In the end, making a budget and saving is not easy, but it is necessary if you want to achieve your goals!"

abroad. For example, a small boutique company in Alabama specializes in creating handmade gowns. But the fine yarn for some of the dresses cannot be found in the United States, so the manufacturer gets it from Turkey. Because the gowns are stitched in the United States, they can legally bear a *Made in USA* label. And that shiny new American car on the showroom floor may actually have been made in Canada or Mexico.

"The U.S. economy is no longer an autonomous entity," says Heather, a Connecticut teenager, on the website of *Teen Ink* magazine. "Rather it is increasingly part of a globally based economy." How can teens take advantage of this new global marketplace? Increasing financial literacy is an important first step. According to the news program *PBS Newshour,* a 2012 study of fifteen-year-olds worldwide showed that US teens ranked in the middle of the scale of financial literacy, below Poland and Latvia, and much lower than the top-rated teens in China. The study confirms that financial literacy is an "essential life skill, and high on the global policy agenda." Learning more about how international commerce works can help teens develop smart buying habits and participate intelligently in the global economy.

> "The value of financial education can't be understated. . . . Most young people have adopted the financial behavior of their parents, who also never formally learned about personal finance in their school years. That's a recipe for disaster."
>
> —Credit counselor Christopher Viale

The global economy also has an impact on US employment. Companies looking to hire the best and brightest new employees no longer look just within the country for suitable candidates. Advances in technology have made numerous jobs obsolete, but at the same time they have created many new opportunities for those with the proper education. Teenagers must take this new world of work into account when choosing a college major or deciding to learn a sought-after skill at a community college.

Credit, Debt, and Your Future

The teen and young adult years are a critical time in building the foundation for a financially secure life. As high school student Amy relates in *The Complete Guide to Personal Finance for Teenagers and College Students,*

"It's an exciting, and also somewhat frightening, time when you begin taking control of your own finances." For a teenager, the future can seem a long way off, but the rewards of getting an early start in financial planning are worth taking time to consider what he or she envisions life could be like in the years ahead.

Becoming educated in the workings of personal finance is essential for today's teenagers, especially since many teens cannot look to their parents to provide good financial role models. "The value of financial education can't be understated," says credit counselor Christopher Viale on CreditCards.com. "Until now, most young people have adopted the financial behavior of their parents, who also never formally learned about personal finance in their school years. That's a recipe for disaster." Financial literacy courses can be found through online searches and by contacting local community colleges or counseling services.

The ability to obtain credit will always be an important part of adult life. Unfortunately, the possibility of getting into too much debt is a danger that is always lurking behind a credit card or loan. Starting with just one credit card in the teen years and making prompt payments on it is an ideal way to begin to build a solid base of good credit. Keeping track of expenses with a budget or other method will help to avoid falling into debt that could spiral out of control and affect future creditworthiness. Recognizing the difference between needs and wants, and controlling impulse spending, are valuable monetary strategies that should be learned and practiced early. For the teenager, good money habits formed today can make all the difference in creating a better life tomorrow.

Glossary

annual percentage rate (APR): The amount of interest a lender charges for a loan over a period of one year, expressed as a percentage.

bankruptcy: A legal proceeding allowing individuals and businesses to declare they cannot repay their debts, often with a court-ordered plan to make partial repayment.

budget: A plan created by an individual, family, or company to manage income and expenses, create financial goals, and make plans to achieve those goals.

collateral: Something of value that is held until a debt is paid. If the debt is not repaid, the collateral can be sold to recover the amount of the loan.

credit: The economic system of allowing customers to make purchases now and pay for them at a future date, usually with interest.

credit history: The record of buying and borrowing habits, used by lenders to evaluate a person's expected ability to repay a loan or credit card charge.

credit limit: The maximum amount that can be charged on a credit card. Going over the credit limit will generate a fee.

debt: An amount of money owed to a person, business, or financial institution.

interest: A percentage added to a loan or a purchase made on credit that compensates the lender for allowing someone to use his or her money.

loan: Money given to someone with the expectation that the amount will be repaid.

overdraft: When more money is withdrawn from a savings or checking account than is in the account.

secured credit card: A credit card that is backed by a savings or checking account as collateral. The amount in the account becomes the credit limit of the card.

unsecured loan: A loan that is not guaranteed by collateral but only by the borrower's promise to repay.

For More Information

Books

Karen Bellenir, ed., *Debt Information for Teens*. Detroit: Omnigraphics, 2011.

Tamsen Butler, *The Complete Guide to Personal Finance for Teenagers and College Students*. Ocala, FL: Atlantic, 2016.

Kathryn R. Deering, ed., *Cash and Credit Information for Teens*. Detroit: Omnigraphics, 2005.

Kara McGuire, *The Teen Money Manual: A Guide to Cash, Credit, Spending, Saving, Work, Wealth, and More*. North Mankato, MN: Capstone, 2015.

Periodicals and Internet Sources

Disease Called Debt (blog), "Debt and Depression: My Personal Experience." http://diseasecalleddebt.com/debt-and-depression.

Colleen Oakley, "You Did What to Pay Off Your Student Loans?," Learnvest, August 8, 2013. www.learnvest.com/2013/08/you-did-what-to-pay-off-your-student-loans.

Jeanine Skowronski, "More Millennials Saying 'No' to Credit Cards," Fox Business, September 18, 2014.

Geoff Williams, "The Hidden Cost of Buying a Car," *U.S. News & World Report Money* (blog), February 13, 2014. http://money.usnews.com/money/personal-finance/articles/2014/02/13/the-hidden-costs-of-buying-a-car.

Websites

Annual Credit Report (www.annualcreditreport.com). Order annual credit reports free of charge from all three reporting agencies from this site.

Consumer Financial Protection Bureau (www.consumerfinance.gov). This site features tools to help prospective college students make informed decisions on paying for college.

Federal Deposit Insurance Corporation Learning Bank (www.fdic.gov/about/learn/learning). This government webpage contains information on various aspects of finance for teens, including links to money management tips and podcasts.

Federal Trade Commission (www.ftc.gov). Learn all about scams, fraud, identity theft, and other vital information for consumers of all ages.

Teens Guide to Money (www.teensguidetomoney. com). A site that helps teens learn about all aspects of finances.

TheMint (www.themint.org). An interactive site that helps teens prepare for making smart financial decisions.

Online Tools, Games, and Apps

Financial Entertainment (http://financialentertainment. org). This website features the games *Celebrity Calamity* and *Bite Nightclub* to teach teens about money management and debt.

JA High School (http://games-juniorachievement-org. s3-website-us-west-2.amazonaws.com/courseware/ Save_USA_2011_HighSchool/launcher.html). A Junior Achievement game that teaches teens about financial planning, setting priorities, and budgeting.

Nerdwallet (www.nerdwallet.com/credit-cards). This online tool compares credit cards according to several categories, including one specifically for students.

Practical Money Skills (www.practicalmoneyskills.com /games). This site has several exciting games that put financial skills to the test. They include *Financial Football, Financial Soccer, Cash Puzzler,* and *Road Trip*.

Schwab Moneywise (www.schwabmoneywise.com/ public/moneywise/calculators_tool). This site provides several online tools, including a credit card payoff calculator, a cost-of-debt calculator, and a college savings calculator.

Start Here, Go Places (www.startheregoplaces.com/ students). This site allows prospective college students to enter criteria to locate a suitable college or university. It also includes the game *Bank on It,* which was created by students for students and lets players deal with finances using real-world scenarios.

Spendee (www.spendeeapp.com). Where has all the money gone at the end of the month? This free iPhone and Android app answers that question with graphs and budgeting tools.

Index